TIRED OF TRYING STUDY GUIDE

TYNDALE
MOMENTUM®

A Tyndale nonfiction imprint

STUDY GUIDE

TIRED OF TRYING
TIRED OF TRYIN
TIRED OF TRYI
TIRED OF TRY
TIRED OF TR
TIRED OF T
TIRED OF
TIRED O
TIRED

FOUR WEEKS OF HOLDING ON TO GOD WHEN YOU'RE FRUSTRATED, FED UP & FEELING FORGOTTEN

ASHLEY MORGAN JACKSON

Visit Tyndale online at tyndale.com.

Visit Tyndale Momentum online at tyndalemomentum.com.

Tyndale, Tyndale's quill logo, *Tyndale Momentum*, and the Tyndale Momentum logo are registered trademarks of Tyndale House Ministries. Tyndale Momentum is a nonfiction imprint of Tyndale House Publishers, Carol Stream, Illinois.

Tired of Trying Study Guide: Four Weeks of Holding On to God When You're Frustrated, Fed Up, and Feeling Forgotten

Cover design and handwritten subtitle by Eva M. Winters.

Edited by Christine M. Anderson

For information about special discounts for bulk purchases, please contact Tyndale House Publishers at csresponse@tyndale.com, or call 1-855-277-9400.

ISBN 979-8-4005-0352-8

Printed in the United States of America

31 30 29 28 27 26 25
7 6 5 4 3 2 1

CONTENTS

A NOTE FROM ASHLEY MORGAN JACKSON

Sometimes we go through seasons in life when every single thing feels so hard that we can't help but wonder, *Where is God? I've loved Him and tried my best to faithfully serve Him, so why isn't He fixing things? Why is He allowing it to hurt so much?* We reason that maybe if we prayed more, studied the Bible more, or worked harder, God would rescue us. But when nothing we do seems to work, we find ourselves at a dead end. We are tired of trying.

You might be in a tired of trying season if you . . .

- feel stuck;
- are grieving the death of a dream;
- feel overlooked or left behind;
- are facing a crisis you never saw coming;
- have an unexpected broken heart;
- are exhausted from an everyday burden; or
- are in a wait that never seems to end.

It is in these seasons that God invites us to wrestle with Him—to bring to Him all our questions, hurts, and doubts, and to hold on to Him with everything we have. The kind of wrestle God invites us to is not quick or easy, but it does have a good purpose—one we may not experience any other way.

I know this wrestle well. There was a season when I wondered if I was the only one who felt crushed by life. Tears rolled down my cheeks constantly as I battled severe anxiety and depression on top of difficult financial and personal circumstances. I hated what my family and I were walking through. I hated that no one seemed to care. And if I'm honest, I hated myself.

One day, I was sitting on the floor in our bedroom when my three-year-old son climbed up on my lap and began singing, "Jesus loves me this I know, for the Bible tells me so. Little ones to Him belong; they are weak, but He is strong."

More tears fell as I knew it was the Lord speaking to me, reminding me that He was with me. He had the strength I didn't have. And He loved me, even though I felt beaten down and exhausted. He invited me to wrestle with Him in the midst of my brokenness and unanswered questions.

If you can relate to this kind of emotional and spiritual exhaustion, it may be that God is inviting you to a wrestle as well. If you're willing to hold on to God, this study will guide you through your wrestling process.

Drawing on the biblical story of Jacob, you'll learn how to

- break out of the cycle of feeling frustrated and stuck;
- identify and act on the hard choices God may be inviting you to make;
- wrestle well with God by holding on to Him even when it's hard; and
- persevere to receive the blessing God has for you on the other side of the wrestle.

We have a choice when we're struggling and tired of trying—we can run toward God or run away from God. My prayer is that you will choose to run toward Him so you can discover God's goodness through it all and receive the blessings He has for you. I believe the Lord has so much He wants to give you as you navigate your hard season. I pray this study will be a vehicle through which you are reminded, "Jesus loves me this I know, for the Bible tells me so."

Ashley Morgan Jackson

STUDY GUIDE OVERVIEW

This study guide and video curriculum are based on the book *Tired of Trying: How to Hold On to God When You're Frustrated, Fed Up, and Feeling Forgotten*. As you progress through the study, you'll see that the theme of Week 1 is based on the introduction to the book, and Weeks 2–4 each align with the three parts of the book. Although the study does not cover all the material in the book chapter by chapter, it does explore the key themes of each part.

Each of the four weeks features a group study and a personal study.

Group Study

The *Tired of Trying* video series and study guide are structured for use in a group setting (such as a small group gathering or Sunday school class) but can also be adapted for individual study. Group sessions are designed to be completed in seventy-five minutes and include five sections: welcome or connection time, video teaching, group discussion, loving and supporting one another, and personal takeaway. Groups are encouraged to close each meeting in prayer. While each section indicates a suggested number of minutes, feel free to adjust the times or otherwise adapt the format to meet the needs of your group or for individual use.

Everyone in the group should have their own copy of this study guide as well as the *Tired of Trying* book. This enables all members to actively engage in group discussions, complete the personal studies between meetings, and benefit from the content in the book. Chapters in the book are designed to be read prior to the group meeting as follows:

IN PREPARATION FOR...	READ...
Week 1: An Invitation to the Wrestle	The book introduction, "An Invitation to the Wrestle"
Week 2: Hard Choices	Chapters 1–4
Week 3: Struggling with God	Chapters 5–8
Week 4: The Blessings of Being Broken	Chapters 9–11

Groups should have a facilitator to help create and maintain a safe environment in which questions, doubts, concerns, struggles, and victories are all welcome. The facilitator is responsible for leading the meeting, starting the video, and keeping track of time during discussions. Facilitators may also prompt participants to contribute to ensure that everyone has the opportunity to engage.

Personal Study

Every group session is followed by a personal study designed to lead participants into a deeper reflection on the theme of that session. Personal studies are to be completed individually between group sessions, and they include a mix of reflection questions, Scripture engagement, application questions, and guided prayers.

When we reach the place where the only choice is to run to God or run from Him, God invites us to hold on to Him even tighter—to wrestle with Him.

Tired of Trying, xvii

Week 1

AN INVITATION TO THE WRESTLE

Welcome

Welcome to Week 1 of the *Tired of Trying* video study. Each session includes reading chapters from the *Tired of Trying* book, a group discussion, and a personal study. As preparation for Week 1, read "An Invitation to the Wrestle," the introduction from the *Tired of Trying* book.

Video: *An Invitation to the Wrestle* (12 minutes)

Play the video for Week 1. As you watch, use the outline below to follow along or to take additional notes.

Notes

- You're not doing anything wrong, and God doesn't love you less because things aren't easy right now.

- Whatever it is that's left you tired of trying may be God's way of inviting you to wrestle with Him.

- The invitation to wrestle with God happens whenever we feel disillusioned, disappointed, or abandoned by Him because our hard seasons persist despite our best efforts to change them. We accept God's invitation to wrestle when we choose to hold on to Him even when we're scared, even when we're tired, and even when we may never have the answers to our questions.

- The roots of Jacob's tired of trying situation go all the way back to before he was even born (Genesis 25:19-27).

▶ Here are two steps to accept the invitation to wrestle:

Step 1: Stop trying and cry out to God for help.

Jacob prays, "Save me . . . from the hand of my brother Esau, for I am afraid he will come and attack me, and also the mothers with their children" (Genesis 32:11).

Jacob knew all his trying wasn't enough; he needed to let go—to *stop trying* what he hoped would work—and instead cry out to God for help.

When we hit the bottom of ourselves, the only direction we can look is up. We need to let go of our own best plans and cry out for God's help. That's how we take the first step to accept His invitation to the wrestle.

Step 2: Accept the process God offers.

Scripture says that after he sent his family and possessions ahead of him, he "was left alone, and a man wrestled with him till daybreak" (Genesis 32:24).*

Jacob prayed to be rescued, but God showed up to wrestle instead. And Jacob had to decide whether to accept God's process.

Are we willing to accept God's terms even when He doesn't show up in the way we would like? And are we willing to allow God to pull us in close, to wrestle with us, no matter how uncomfortable it makes us?

* To learn more about why God is described in this verse as "a man," see the *Tired of Trying* book, page 63.

Here's the thing about any kind of wrestling—it's not possible to do it from a safe distance. It requires direct contact with an opponent.

▶ If our good God invites us to wrestle, He *will* bring us through it.

▶ Real life is complicated—it's hard—and we have a choice: Will we go through our hard season with God or without Him?

► ***This week:*** Every time you start to feel overwhelmed by the pain that has you feeling so tired, say to yourself, "God doesn't need me to figure everything out; He only expects me to trust Him one step at a time."

Group Discussion (51 minutes)

1. What part of the video teaching resonated most with you?

2. Which of the following best describes how you feel when you are tired of trying?

   ☐ *I try harder to fix things on my own.* I must have not been doing enough to begin with.

   ☐ *I go numb.* If there is no solution, I protect myself by trying not to feel at all.

   ☐ *I get frustrated.* I think, "Why can't I figure this out? Whose fault is it? Hurry up!"

   ☐ *I distract myself.* I get busy with other things to keep my mind off it.

   ☐ *I pretend.* I try to fake my way through, even if I'm dying inside.

   ☐ *I withdraw.* No one needs to know because they won't care anyway.

   ☐ Other:

3. The invitation to wrestle with God happens whenever we feel disillusioned, disappointed, or abandoned by Him because our hard seasons persist despite our best efforts to change them. Which of these feelings, if any, do you have toward God right now? If you feel comfortable doing so, share the reasons for your response.

4. Jacob's life was filled with years of family drama and dysfunction, including cheating his brother, Esau, tricking his father, Isaac, and spending two decades in exile. Eventually, God called him back to his homeland to face his past, but he was full of fear because he didn't know if Esau still wanted to kill him. So Jacob did something we can probably all relate to: He tried really hard to fix things on his own.

> Jacob sent messengers ahead of him to his brother Esau in the land of Seir, the country of Edom. He instructed them: "This is what you are to say to my lord Esau: 'Your servant Jacob says, I have been staying with Laban and have remained there till now. I have cattle and donkeys, sheep and goats, male and female servants. Now I am sending this message to my lord, that I may find favor in your eyes.'"
>
> When the messengers returned to Jacob, they said, "We went to your brother Esau, and now he is coming to meet you, and four hundred men are with him."
>
> In great fear and distress Jacob divided the people who were with him into two groups, and the flocks and herds and camels as well. He thought, "If Esau comes and attacks one group, the group that is left may escape."
>
> GENESIS 32:3-8

- How would you characterize Jacob's efforts to fix and control his circumstances? For example, what tactics did he use? On whom or on what was he focused?

- In what ways, if any, do you relate to Jacob's response? For example, what tactics do you tend to rely on to fix or control things when you are scared or overwhelmed? On whom or on what do you tend to focus? Do you focus on yourself, the problem, your circumstances, others, God?

5. Despite doing everything he could to fix things, Jacob soon realized that his situation was more overwhelming than his plans could manage. When he came to the end of himself, he took the first step to accept God's invitation to wrestle by crying out to God for help.

> Then Jacob prayed, "O God of my father Abraham, God of my father Isaac, LORD, you who said to me, 'Go back to your country and your relatives, and I will make you prosper,' I am unworthy of all the kindness and faithfulness you have shown your servant. I had only my staff when I crossed this Jordan, but now I have become two camps. Save me, I pray, from the hand of my brother Esau, for I am afraid he will come and attack me, and also the mothers with their children. But you have said, 'I will surely make you prosper and will make your descendants like the sand of the sea, which cannot be counted.'"
>
> GENESIS 32:9-12

- In what ways might Jacob's prayer hint at the physical wrestle with God that is to come? In other words, how does he both challenge God and hold on to God in his prayer?

- How do you respond to the idea of both challenging God and holding on to God in your own prayers? In what ways does it encourage you? In what ways do you find this difficult?

6. When we come to the end of ourselves, the first step in accepting God's invitation to wrestle is to *stop trying*—to let go of trying to fix and control things and instead cry out for God's help.

   Which of the following statements best describes your initial reaction to this idea that we need to stop trying when we come to the end of ourselves? Share the reason for your choice.

   - ☐ It feels wrong and even irresponsible.
   - ☐ It feels scary because I don't know what God will ask me to do.
   - ☐ It feels frustrating. My way seems reasonable and even godly.
   - ☐ It feels uncertain but somehow also like a relief because it takes the pressure off me.
   - ☐ It feels needed. I recognize I need help.

7. As much as Jacob may have hoped God would intervene and save him from his circumstances, the only thing God offered was a long wrestle. That's when Jacob faced his second step—he had to decide whether to accept the process God offered.

   What comes to mind when you imagine accepting God's process for your own situation? What might it mean for you to allow God to pull you in close so you can wrestle together through your fears and frustrations?

Loving and Supporting One Another (10 minutes)

Use one or more of the statements below to share how the group can best love and support you throughout this study.

- ☐ *The area of my life in which I feel most tired of trying right now is* _______________. (Examples: my marriage, my wandering kids, my finances, my mental health, etc.) *You can help me best by* _______________.
- ☐ *I would feel most supported in this group if you* _______________. (Examples: just listen, offer words of encouragement, reach out to me between sessions, pray for me, etc.)
- ☐ *One thing that would make me withdraw or share less is* _______________. (Examples: criticism, even if constructive; minimizing my pain; being misunderstood or judged; not being asked for my input; etc.)
- ☐ *One word or phrase that describes what I would like to experience in this group is* _______________. (Examples: feeling understood and accepted, feeling less alone, hope, purpose, peace, etc.)

Personal Takeaway (2 minutes)

What stood out most to you from the teaching or discussion? Use the space below to write down your personal takeaway.

My takeaway from this week's session:

Closing Prayer

WEEK 1 PERSONAL STUDY

When we're tired of trying, we feel overwhelmed by emotions. For some, it may be discouragement, resentment, or hopelessness. For others, it might be frustration at the lack of solutions, fear that this season will never end, or feeling like maybe God has forgotten us as our prayers seemed to be going nowhere. Everything matters, and yet somehow, we begin to feel like nothing matters.

> **"I wanted [God] to get me back to the girl I once was. I wanted Him to help me become the strong version of myself that was respected and much easier to love. Why wasn't He doing what I so desperately wanted Him to do? I wrestled between feeling like God had hurt my feelings and knowing that wasn't possible. An ache shot through me as I wondered how I could feel so betrayed by a God I loved so much."**
>
> *Tired of Trying*, xv

1. Even though we know God is perfect and would never do anything to harm us, one of the hardest parts of being tired of trying is feeling let down by God, like He hasn't kept His side of the bargain.

   In what ways do you feel that God has let you down or perhaps even betrayed you?

   What questions do you have for God or about God as a result?

2. In your Bible, read Genesis 32:3-24. Consider the events leading up to Jacob's wrestle.

    What do you relate to most about Jacob's circumstances, his fears, or his efforts to fix things on his own?

"Like Jacob, when we are in our deepest pain, we can choose to hang on to our good and capable God as we boldly cry out for help. As we wrestle, we learn how to let go of our need to perform for God and discover how to let Him love us just as we are—fears, frustrations, and all. The Lord can do more with our honest pleas for help than our forced performances. Sometimes the best prayers we can pray are the simple ones: 'This hurts. I'm scared. Please help.'"

Tired of Trying, xix

3. Just as Jacob had to stop trying and cry out to God about what he was going through, so do we. We can be honest with God about our broken hearts, our wounds, and our deep fears and frustrations. In fact, we must. Otherwise, we will continue to place the burden of our struggles on our own backs, which is why we are so tired of trying in the first place. We were never made to figure everything out on our own.

   What, if anything, has led you to try and do everything on your own—to withhold yourself from God or to avoid being completely honest with Him about what you're going through?

4. After he cried out to God for help, Jacob had to surrender to what God offered him in that moment, which was a long wrestle. Use the space below to share your heart with God—your wounds, fears, questions, and frustrations. Ask for His help, being specific about what you need from Him. Then express your willingness (or unwillingness) to surrender to His good plans for you. Even in this, He is for you.

Up Next

In preparation for Week 2, read chapters 1–4 in *Tired of Trying*.

God is not in a rush. He does not shame you for being where you are. He is with you in your dark night as you make these hard choices.

Tired of Trying, 75

Week 2

TIRED

HARD CHOICES

Connection Time (10 minutes)

Touch base with one another about what you learned and experienced over the past week.

- What was it like to practice saying to yourself, "God doesn't need me to figure everything out; He only expects me to trust Him one step at a time"?

- What insights stood out to you from the Week 1 personal study?

Video: *Hard Choices* (14 minutes)

Play the video for Week 2. As you watch, use the outline below to follow along or to take additional notes.

Notes

- The dictionary defines *stuck* as being unable to move, unable to make progress, or unable to find solutions.[1]

- When Jacob knew he was stuck, he realized he had to make a hard choice, and the same is true for us when we feel stuck.

▶ Here are three things Jacob did—and we can do—to get unstuck:

1. Recognize the indicators of the hard choice.

The first thing Jacob did was recognize the indicators that he was facing a hard choice—that he had to do something.

Indicators are the difficult feelings we begin to notice when we struggle with something again and again.

Jacob's primary indicator was frustration.

Because indicators are the symptoms of something we need to address to get unstuck, they might come in any number of forms. For example:

- when we're frustrated
- when God hurts our feelings
- when God reveals unhealthy roots
- when we can no longer pretend

2. Name the hard choice.

It wasn't until Jacob explained the situation to his wives that he said the hard part out loud: "Your father's attitude toward me is not what it was before. . . . You know that I've worked for your father with all my strength, yet your father has cheated me by changing my wages ten times" (Genesis 31:5-7). In other words, "We have to make a hard choice about whether to stay or go."

Rachel and Leah responded, "Do whatever God has told you" (Genesis 31:16). In other words, "Make the hard choice."

Sometimes when we come to a point in our lives where we need to do something different, we try to avoid it rather than face it.

Once we recognize our indicators, chances are we will begin to see our hard choices more clearly—we just need the courage to name them.

3. Make the hard choice to surrender to God's plan.

"Jacob put his children and his wives on camels, and he drove all his livestock ahead of him . . . to go to his father Isaac in the land of Canaan" (Genesis 31:17-18).

We make the hard choice to surrender to God's plan when we admit that our way isn't working and that, even if we don't know how it will all work out, we are willing to do it His way.

Sometimes, like Jacob, we receive clear direction from the Lord of what to do next. With all the faith we have, we begin to move toward surrender, one step at a time.

Other times, surrender may mean agreeing to what God wants us to do even if His will is not clear yet.

God wants us to face our hard choices, but He doesn't expect us to figure everything out on our own.

► ***This week:*** Follow Jacob's example by recognizing your indicators and naming one hard choice God may be inviting you to make. Explore what surrendering that hard choice to God might look like. You don't have to take action if you're not ready. Simply do your best to identify what your next step might be.

Group Discussion (40 minutes)

1. What part of the video teaching resonated most with you?

2. Sometimes feeling stuck looks like remaining in a negative pattern of thought or behavior we can't seem to escape. Which of the patterns below feels most familiar to you?

   - ☐ believing God *can* step in but probably won't
   - ☐ feeling so unsure of what to do next that I become paralyzed and do nothing
   - ☐ believing lies about myself (*I'm unworthy, unwanted, unqualified*, etc.)
   - ☐ fearing rejection from God or others
   - ☐ feeling like I am always letting people down
   - ☐ carrying too much on my own and getting overwhelmed again and again
   - ☐ other:

3. Our negative patterns are often indicators or signs pointing to hard choices God might be asking us to make.

   - In what ways, if any, have you experienced this dynamic in the past? For example, what were your indicators and hard choices? How did you respond?

- Based on your experiences, why do you think we often choose to stay in negative patterns, ignoring the indicators?

4. Jacob got to the point where he could no longer ignore that living with and working for his father-in-law was becoming harder and harder. It was at this point that the Lord said to him, "Return to the land of your fathers and to your kindred, and I will be with you" (Genesis 31:3, ESV).

    - How do you think God may have used Jacob's circumstances to prepare him for the hard choice he needed to make?

- God told Jacob to do something that was hard and scary, but He also reassured Jacob by promising, "I will be with you." Instead of changing Jacob's circumstances, God promised to be with Jacob in them. What comes to mind when you imagine God making the same promise to you for whatever circumstances or hard choices you may be facing? How might this promise change your perspective?

5. When Jacob found himself between a rock and a hard place, he had two choices: He could stay in the situation with Laban and continue to struggle, or he could make the hard choice to obey God and return to his homeland. With certain hardship behind him and fear of his brother, Esau, before him, he told Leah and Rachel:

> I see that your father's attitude toward me is not what it was before, but the God of my father has been with me. You know that I've worked for your father with all my strength, yet your father has cheated me by changing my wages ten times. However, God has not allowed him to harm me.
>
> GENESIS 31:5-7

Rachel and Leah responded, "Do whatever God has told you" (Genesis 31:16).

- Based on the passage, how would you describe the role that God played in Jacob's hardships? What did God do and not do?

- How would you describe Jacob's statement to Rachel and Leah? For example, what did he say and not say about his circumstances? About God?

- Once Jacob said the hard part out loud, Rachel and Leah fully supported him. In what ways, if any, have you experienced something similar? Can you recall a time when the act of naming your hard choice brought unexpected peace, support, or courage?

6. When we feel stuck, we wrestle with God because we think we know the best way to fix things. If God would only take our suggestions, we believe everything would turn out well. But just as He did with Jacob, God often wants us to take a first step without knowing how everything will turn out. Making hard choices always requires trusting God.

Listed below are four verses about trusting God. Go around the group and read each one aloud.

> Trust in the LORD with all your heart, and do not lean on your own understanding.
>
> PROVERBS 3:5, ESV

> When I am afraid, I put my trust in you. In God, whose word I praise, in God I trust; I shall not be afraid. What can flesh do to me?
>
> PSALM 56:3-4, ESV

> Commit your way to the LORD; trust in him, and he will act.
>
> PSALM 37:5, ESV

> You will keep in perfect peace all who trust in you, all whose thoughts are fixed on you!
>
> ISAIAH 26:3, NLT

- Which verse *challenges* you most about trusting God in the circumstances or hard choices you're facing?

- Which verse *encourages* you most about trusting God in the circumstances or hard choices you're facing?

Loving and Supporting One Another (9 minutes)

Use one or more of the statements below to share how the group can best pray for you between now and next week.

- ☐ Pray that God would reveal to me the areas in which I may be stuck without yet realizing it.
- ☐ Ask God to give me insight and wisdom to identify the hard choices I may need to make.
- ☐ Pray that God would give me courage to make the hard choice He's already asked me to make.
- ☐ Ask God to increase my trust—that I would be able to take the next steps even when His ways are not my ways and I don't know how things will turn out.
- ☐ Other:

Personal Takeaway (2 minutes)

What stood out most to you from the teaching or discussion? Use the space below to write down your personal takeaway.

My takeaway from this week's session:

Closing Prayer

WEEK 2 PERSONAL STUDY

There are times in our lives when we feel stuck—when nothing we have tried, nothing we have prayed, and nothing we have done to avoid or escape our problems has worked. We can't help but wonder, *Why isn't anything helping?* But when God comes to wrestle with us, His intentions are always to set us free. Sometimes the first step to getting unstuck is being willing to see our situation from God's perspective and letting Him have His way, which is always for our good.

> **"All the strategies that I'd used in the past led only to dead ends. *Was it something I was doing, not doing, had done? Was this from sin? Was this a punishment? Was God mad at me?* If only I could figure out how to learn the lesson I was supposed to learn from this season, then maybe I could be free of it."**
>
> *Tired of Trying*, 6

1. When we feel stuck and tired of trying, it's often because we have been doing our utmost to solve our problems on our own or to come up with another strategy for getting ourselves out of whatever messes we're in.

   What strategies have you used in an attempt to fix, avoid, or escape the circumstances or struggles that have you feeling stuck and tired of trying?

What tender questions, concerns, or difficult emotions are you wrestling with because your strategies are not working?

2. Indicators are the difficult feelings we notice when we struggle with something repeatedly. They *indicate* that we are facing a hard choice. The chart on the following pages summarizes four common indicators we might experience when we feel stuck. Read through the descriptions and use the right column on the chart to note the ways in which you relate to or recognize each indicator in your own life.

INDICATORS *(Indicators are symptoms of an issue that needs to be addressed to get unstuck.)*	**WAYS IN WHICH I RELATE TO OR RECOGNIZE THIS INDICATOR**
I am frustrated. I am upset or annoyed because of my inability to change or achieve something. My frustration shows up as anger, getting busy and trying harder, sadness, depression, or numbing out to avoid the pain of feeling stuck and not having answers.	
God has hurt my feelings. I am struggling because God has allowed something to happen in my life that has hurt me deeply. I know He is perfect and doesn't intend to hurt me, but I feel crushed about the response or lack of response from Him about my circumstances.	
God has revealed unhealthy roots. I am struggling with self-defeating patterns of belief that drive my behaviors and therefore my life. These patterns often take the form of self-accusations or lies about myself or God. For example, sometimes I feel like I'm not good enough, people don't like me, I am way too much but never enough, or that God is tired of me and my problems.	

INDICATORS *(Indicators are symptoms of an issue that needs to be addressed to get unstuck.)*	**WAYS IN WHICH I RELATE TO OR RECOGNIZE THIS INDICATOR**
I can no longer pretend. I have been putting on a brave and faithful face, but I no longer have the capacity to pretend I'm "fine" when I'm not. I'm tired of having to perform to earn acceptance from God, others, and even myself.	
Other:	

> **"As much as it might hurt to hear, I think deep down we all know that God's number one goal in our lives is not to give us what we want, but to make us more like Christ. And one of the ways that happens is when we make choices that aren't always easy."**
>
> *Tired of Trying*, 26

3. Briefly review what you wrote on the chart and circle the indicator you relate to most.

   If an indicator is a symptom, what comes to mind when you consider the potential cause of your symptom(s)? In other words, what is wrong that needs to be addressed?

What hard choice or choices might you need to make to address what's wrong?

"When God invites us to wrestle with Him, He is looking for our surrender—for our willingness to let Him do what He wants to do in our lives. . . . When we give up control, we allow a God who is much wiser than us to be in charge."

Tired of Trying, 40

4. Making hard choices requires surrender. The enemy wants us to believe that surrendering to God is not for our benefit. And yet, when we surrender to God—when we seek His way first—we are not defeated but empowered. God's promise to us is this: "Seek first the kingdom of God and his righteousness, and all these things will be added to you" (Matthew 6:33, ESV).

   What comes to mind when you consider what surrendering your hard choice to God might look like? What, specifically, might you have to let go of?

   In what ways do you hope surrendering to God might empower you or help you to get unstuck?

5. When we begin to surrender and make the hard choices God is asking us to make, we are choosing to audaciously hold on to God. It is through this process that He reveals who He is, why He can be trusted, and how He is blessing you with more freedom. Write out an honest prayer to God, asking Him to help you make the hard choices that may lie in front of you.

Up Next

In preparation for Week 3, read chapters 5–8 in *Tired of Trying*.

Imagine daring to believe that on the other side of this wrestle and struggle is a faith that is much deeper and far less shakable.

Tired of Trying, 104

Week 3

TIRED

STRUGGLING WITH GOD

Connection Time (10 minutes)

Touch base with one another about what you learned and experienced over the past week.

- What was it like to recognize the indicators in your life and to name one hard choice God may be inviting you to take?

- What insights stood out to you from the Week 2 personal study?

Video: *Struggling with God* (13 minutes)

Play the video for Week 3. As you watch, use the outline below to follow along or to take additional notes.

Notes

- We wrestle with God when we choose to go to Him with our disillusionment, disappointment, or dread.

- Jacob has made the hard choice to return to his homeland and is about to face his brother, Esau.

▶ "So Jacob was left alone, and a man wrestled with him till daybreak. When the man saw that he could not overpower him, he touched the socket of Jacob's hip so that his hip was wrenched as he wrestled with the man. Then the man said, 'Let me go, for it is daybreak.' But Jacob replied, 'I will not let you go unless you bless me'" (Genesis 32:24-26).

▶ On the eve of facing his greatest fear, Jacob prayed for God to save him, and God's answer to that prayer was a wrestle. Yet God used this wrestle to both change and bless Jacob in ways he could not have experienced otherwise.

► Here are three things we can learn from Jacob that will help us when we wrestle with God:

1. Wrestling with God is long and hard.

Jacob wrestled with God all night. That's a long time to hold on to an opponent, a long time to use every ounce of strength to win, a long time to not give up.

Sometimes the long struggle itself *is* the lesson we need to learn.

"We rejoice in our sufferings, knowing that suffering produces endurance, and endurance produces character, and character produces hope" (Romans 5:3-4, ESV).

We don't endure for the sake of endurance alone; we endure because it produces good fruit within us—character and hope.

2. Wrestling with God hurts.

Jacob was physically wounded when the Lord wrenched his hip (Genesis 32:25).

When we hold on to God even when it hurts, we will walk away from that encounter knowing Him more intimately than we ever have before.

3. *Wrestling with God has a purpose.*

God wrestled with Jacob not to harm him but to bless him.

"The man asked him, 'What is your name?' 'Jacob,' he answered. Then the man said, 'Your name will no longer be Jacob, but Israel, because you have struggled with God and with humans and have overcome'" (Genesis 32:27-28).

Jacob couldn't walk into a new future with an old identity; he had to know who God had called him to be.

God is willing to wrestle with us until we walk away changed.

► ***This week:*** Identify one way you can hold on to God in the middle of your wrestle. Maybe it's praying even when you aren't sure what to pray for. Maybe it's doing your personal study even though, if you're honest, you'd rather avoid God because you feel like He's hurt your feelings. Maybe it's asking God to show you how to surrender to Him.

Group Discussion (40 minutes)

1. What part of the video teaching resonated most with you?

2. Often we wrestle to get God to do things our way. Which of the reasons below best describes why you sometimes wrestle with God?

   - ☐ I am convinced my way is best.
   - ☐ I get tired of waiting for God to act.
   - ☐ I'm freaking out and desperate for a solution.
   - ☐ It feels unsafe to rely on *trust* when I'm drowning in my problems.
   - ☐ Other:

3. After he sent his family and possessions ahead of him, Scripture says:

> Jacob was left alone, and a man wrestled with him till daybreak. When the man saw that he could not overpower him, he touched the socket of Jacob's hip so that his hip was wrenched as he wrestled with the man. Then the man said, "Let me go, for it is daybreak." But Jacob replied, "I will not let you go unless you bless me."
>
> GENESIS 32:24-26

   - Jacob wrestled alone and in the dark of night. Why do you think God approached Jacob in this way?

- What might Jacob's experience suggest about what we can expect in our own seasons of wrestling with God?

- Jacob had known since he was a child that the Lord planned to give him the blessing that belonged to the oldest son, even though he was the youngest (Genesis 25:23). When that blessing took longer than expected, Jacob and his mother schemed and manipulated to make it happen sooner. And while they technically succeeded, Jacob had to flee the wrath of his brother, Esau, and spend two decades in exile. In this passage, it's clear that Jacob is determined not to be thwarted again, so he demands God's blessing as a condition of his surrender.

  In what ways, if any, do you recognize this aspect of Jacob's story in your life or the lives of others? In other words, how do we sometimes try to "help" God bless us by forcing or manipulating our circumstances to get what we want on our own terms or timetable?

4. Seasons of wrestling with God are often longer and harder than we anticipated. While we prioritize instant answers and relief when we're struggling, God prioritizes the strength that comes from enduring. The apostle Paul writes, "We rejoice in our sufferings, knowing that suffering produces endurance, and endurance produces character, and character produces hope" (Romans 5:3-4, ESV).

   Based on what you've experienced in your own seasons of struggle, consider how you might define each of the words Paul uses. Use the starter sentences below to describe what it looks like in practical terms to experience endurance, character, and hope.

   I know my suffering is producing endurance when . . .

   I know my endurance is producing character when . . .

I know my character is producing hope when . . .

5. Jacob experienced great pain when his hip was put out of joint, and yet he continued to wrestle. Sometimes the pain we experience in wrestling comes when God asks us challenging questions such as, "Who are you really trusting?"

   What questions do you sense God may be asking you as you wrestle with Him? In other words, where is God challenging you in ways that make you uncomfortable?

6. Jacob's wrestle with God had a purpose—to bless him. And the first of those blessings came when God changed his name from Jacob to Israel (Genesis 32:27-28). It is a name change that indicates an identity change—Jacob's endurance has changed his character.

   It's been said that if we are never challenged, we will never be changed. In what ways do you hope God might use your season of wrestling to change you? For example, what negative labels would you like to leave behind? What would you like your new identity to be?

Loving and Supporting One Another (10 minutes)

Use one or more of the statements below to share how the group can best pray for you between now and next week.

- ☐ Pray that I will run *to* God rather than *away* from God in my wrestle.
- ☐ Ask God to give me strength to endure what I am walking through with grace.
- ☐ Pray that I will be willing to embrace what God wants to do in my life, even if it's different from what I want.
- ☐ Ask God to give me eyes to see the good plans He has for me.
- ☐ Other:

Personal Takeaway (2 minutes)

What stood out most to you from the teaching or discussion? Use the space below to write down your personal takeaway.

My takeaway from this week's session:

Closing Prayer

WEEK 3 PERSONAL STUDY

If you need the reminder today, God is not put off by your struggle with Him. In fact, He is always inviting you to bring your heart to Him, even when it's broken. Wrestling with God happens when we are brave enough to bring into His presence the things that are weighing us down and to hold on to Him for dear life. Even when it takes longer than you expected, even when it's more painful than you want it to be, God does have something beautiful for you on the other side of your wrestle. Trust Him.

> **"God could no longer allow self-reliance to continue in Jacob's life—and He can no longer allow it to continue in ours. This, my friend, is when we learn to practice surrender."**
>
> *Tired of Trying*, 88

1. To surrender is "to yield to the power, control, or possession of another upon compulsion or demand," or "to give (oneself) up into the power of another."[2] It's no wonder most of us avoid having anything to do with surrender! Based on this definition, what would you say is the hardest thing for you when it comes to surrendering to God?

2. Jacob was so determined not to surrender as he wrestled with God, that the Lord had to wound him: "When the man saw that he did not prevail against Jacob, he touched his hip socket, and Jacob's hip was put out of joint as he wrestled with him" (Genesis 32:25, ESV). Bible commentators suggest God purposely held back His strength and allowed the wrestle to continue so Jacob would willingly recognize his need to surrender.

   Why do you think it was important for Jacob to willingly surrender? What might the alternative have been?

How do you understand this dynamic in your own life? In what ways, if any, might God be allowing you to come to the end of your own strength as you wrestle with Him?

"God engages us in a wrestle to reveal that there is so much more going on than what we are currently experiencing. His purpose is to reveal Himself to us in a new way. We begin to recognize that all along, it was God Himself that we needed, and that only He can provide the blessing we will walk away with."

Tired of Trying, 102

3. By the end of his wrestle, Jacob was undoubtedly in a lot of pain. Yet, he refused to surrender, saying, "I will not let you go unless you bless me" (Genesis 32:26). This marks a mindset shift for Jacob—he shifted his focus from the wrestle itself to the one with whom he wrestled.

   As you reflect on your own wrestle with God, how do you understand the difference between focusing on the pain of the wrestle and focusing on the one with whom you wrestle?

Speaking of Jacob's wrestle, one Bible commentator writes, "As always, with God one has to lose in order to win."[3] This is a theme Jesus taught when He said, "For whoever wants to save their life will lose it, but whoever loses their life for me will find it" (Matthew 16:25). How might letting go of your way for God's way feel like losing but ultimately be for your good?

"To practice surrender is to acknowledge that we are tired of trying because we were never meant to try so hard in our own strength. God has brought us to this place to show us that He never expected us to figure things out on our own or have what it takes to get through our struggles without Him."

Tired of Trying, 89

4. Surrendering doesn't always come easy, not even when the one to whom we're surrendering is God. But surrender is something we can practice and get better at over time. Use the prompts below to practice surrendering to God in an area of life you're struggling with right now.

The area of life in which I am struggling most to take or keep control is . . .

My fears are . . .

I know I cannot move forward without the Lord's help because . . .

The specific outcomes I am releasing are . . .

The help and strength I need from God are . . .

Use your responses to write a prayer of surrender to God. If you find it helpful, use the following prayer (from page 89 of *Tired of Trying*) as a starting point:

Lord, I recognize I am trying to control ______________________ *because I am afraid* ______________________. *I admit I have tried to overcome this on my own, and I am now fully aware of my weakness. I am asking you, Lord, to please fill me with your strength. I let go of the expectation that the outcomes must be* ______________________ *or turn out like* ______________________. *I have nothing, Lord, but you have everything I need. I am believing by faith that you are even now providing me with your strength and help.*

In Jesus' name, amen.

Up Next

In preparation for Week 4, read chapters 9–11 in *Tired of Trying*.

Soon, we will begin to experience the blessing—our tiredness turns into boldness, our hopelessness becomes overflowing joy, and we know that the wrestle was worth it. We are not the same, and we never will be again.

Tired of Trying, 183

Week 4

THE BLESSINGS OF BEING BROKEN

Connection Time (10 minutes)

Touch base with one another about what you learned and experienced over the past week.

- How did you do with identifying one way you can hold on to God in the middle of your wrestle?

- What insights stood out to you from the Week 3 personal study?

Video: *The Blessings of Being Broken* (14 minutes)

Play the video for Week 4. As you watch, use the outline below to follow along or to take additional notes.

Notes

► Sometimes, the blessings God wants to give us don't look like we might expect. Instead, they may look like the following:

- helping us become who He has called us to be
- teaching us what dependence on Him really looks like
- showing us how to stand on His truth when life is painful
- equipping us to help others

► At the end of his wrestle, Jacob didn't walk away a champion, but he did walk away blessed.

► Here are three examples of what God's blessing looks like:

1. God's blessing looks like being changed.

God says, "Your name is Jacob, but you will no longer be called Jacob; your name will be Israel" (Genesis 35:10). Jacob is no longer defined by a name that evokes his old identity as a cheater and schemer but by a name that means "perseverer with God."[4] Jacob "struggled with God and with humans and [overcame]" (Genesis 32:28). Through his wrestle, God changed Jacob's identity.

When we are in Christ, our identities are not in our struggles but in our relationship to Him and the sacrifice He made at the Cross.

We are covered by His blood, chosen, set apart, and adopted by Him.

The blessing God has for us on the other side of our wrestle is to be changed—to know with certainty who we are and to move forward in that confidence.

2. God's blessing looks like renewed trust.

God required Jacob to face his greatest fear without knowing what the outcome would be, and as Jacob did that, his trust in God was renewed. God's faithfulness hadn't changed, but Jacob's obedience enabled him to experience it in an undeniable way.

The promise of Scripture is that "in all things God works for the good of those who love him, who have been called according to his purpose" (Romans 8:28).

It may take some time and holding on for dear life, but God *will* show us His faithfulness and be there to remind us that He can be trusted with our broken and weary hearts.

3. God's blessing looks like impacting others.

God gives Jacob the promise of even more blessings, telling him to be fruitful and multiply, because "a nation and a community of nations will come from you, and kings will be among your descendants" (Genesis 35:11).

God's blessings are always for us, but not for us alone. He blesses us so we can be a blessing. He gives us the blessings of brokenness so we can pass them along to impact others.

Group Discussion (40 minutes)

1. What part of the video teaching resonated most with you?

2. If you were to post a photo or two to social media using *#blessed*, what images would you use? What pictures would best capture your understanding or hopes of what it means to be blessed?

3. Sometimes our greatest blessings come in packages we would never have asked for or expected. These are the blessings of brokenness. In what ways, if any, have you experienced such blessings in the past?

4. God blesses Jacob at the end of their wrestle by changing his name from Jacob to Israel. Now he is no longer defined by a name that evokes his old identity as a cheater and schemer but by a name that means "perseverer with God."[5] Jacob "struggled with God and with humans and [overcame]" (Genesis 32:28). Commenting on the significance of the name change, Bible scholar John Walton writes, "Changing someone's name was a way to exert authority over a person. Jacob accepts the name change, which in this case is equivalent to accepting a change in character."[6]

   To be changed, Jacob had to accept God's authority over him. How do you understand this dynamic in your own life? What might it mean in practical terms to *accept* a change in character?

5. Jacob prayed for God to save him from Esau, but God far exceeded that prayer by reconciling the brothers instead. Scripture says, "Esau ran to meet Jacob and embraced him; he threw his arms around his neck and kissed him. And they wept" (Genesis 33:4). Jacob, who had fled from his brother's death threats, now embraced him in a miraculous reconciliation.

    - As you reflect on this scene, picture yourself as Jacob, with Esau representing whatever it is you fear most in the difficulties you're facing. What comes to mind when you imagine how God might far exceed your prayers?

- When we're wrestling through hard seasons, we are constantly tempted to think in terms of worst-case scenarios, which means we view the world through fearful and anxious thoughts. In what ways does the miraculous reconciliation of Jacob and Esau challenge your own worst-case-scenario thinking? In what ways does it encourage you?

6. God blesses Jacob at the end of their wrestle but later adds to the blessing, saying, "I am God Almighty; be fruitful and increase in number. A nation and a community of nations will come from you, and kings will be among your descendants" (Genesis 35:11).

   - Eighteenth-century Bible scholar John Gill suggests that using the phrase "I am God Almighty" was God's way of emphasizing that He was able to protect and defend Jacob and fulfill all the promises He had made.[7] How does being reminded of all God is capable of keep our fears in check?

- When God gives us blessings and promises, they are irrevocable. In what ways recently has God reminded you that He is the Almighty—that He has good plans and blessings for you?

Loving and Supporting One Another (9 minutes)

Use one or more of the statements below to share how the group can best pray for you as this study concludes.

☐ Pray that God will reveal to me the blessing He wants to give me through my wrestle.

☐ Ask God to help me say, like Jacob, "I won't let go until you bless me!"

☐ Pray that God would allow me to walk in who He has called me to be.

☐ Ask God to bring the renewed trust I need in Him, others, and even myself.

☐ Other:

Personal Takeaway (2 minutes)

What stood out most to you from the teaching or discussion? Use the space below to write down your personal takeaway.

My takeaway from this week's session:

Closing Prayer

WEEK 4 PERSONAL STUDY

When we're struggling, we want to hurry up and do whatever we can to fix ourselves or our situation. But God is not in a rush. He knows exactly how long our wrestle will take, and He wants us to learn to rely on Him for each moment, to pour out our every question, and to lay our burdens on Him.

Wherever you find yourself today, know that God will never abandon you. As you press into your wrestle and hold on for the blessing, determine in your heart to get to know the one with whom you wrestle. He truly is the greatest blessing you will ever receive.

> **"We are not the faithful ones, He is. This wrestle is His plan and it's His job, as we put our hope in Him, to get us to the other side of this. And sometimes it's in the middle of waiting patiently for the good God is working that we discover God Himself is all we ever really needed."**
>
> *Tired of Trying,* 134

1. Based on the blessings Jacob received through his wrestle, the following chart summarizes three blessings we, too, might receive from our wrestle with God. As you read through the descriptions, use the right column to reflect on how you have experienced or hope to experience these blessings in your life.

THE BLESSINGS OF BROKENNESS	HOW I HAVE EXPERIENCED OR HOPE TO EXPERIENCE THIS BLESSING
The blessing of being changed. The blessing of change is the ability to think differently, believe differently, and respond differently.	
The blessing of renewed trust. The blessing of renewed trust happens as we see the Lord work through our bold steps of obedience. We remember who God is, who we are, and why we can trust Him.	

THE BLESSINGS OF BROKENNESS	HOW I HAVE EXPERIENCED OR HOPE TO EXPERIENCE THIS BLESSING
The blessing of impacting others. The blessing of impacting others is the authority and knowledge we now have so that we can be compassionate friends to those who are hurting. We can encourage them by sharing how God has been faithful to us and will be faithful to them as well.	
Other:	

2. Briefly review what you wrote on the chart and circle the blessing that stands out most to you.

   What is it about this blessing that feels especially significant or meaningful?

   What thoughts or emotions does this blessing make you aware of?

How do you imagine or hope this blessing might impact your future?

> **"When God engages us in a wrestling season, it is not to change our circumstances but to teach us how to deal with each new battle and struggle as we move forward with a new perspective. Our blessing is having been changed from the inside out. So, just as God did with Jacob, He allows us to walk with a limp."**
>
> *Tired of Trying*, 175

3. After Jacob had wrestled and received a blessing from God, he moved on—but not without a bodily reminder of how dependent he was on God (Genesis 32:31). The sun rose on Jacob's life again, and yet he remained marked by his experience. He walked away from his wrestle with a limp, a constant reminder of what he had been through and who he had become.

   In our own lives, to walk with a limp means, in part, that we now bear a mark of both victory and weakness. Our victory is the blessing of transformation God has released through our wrestle, and our weakness is a reminder of our need for God.

   When you reflect on your wrestle, what might you identify as your limp—your mark of both victory and weakness?

In what ways might your limp be a lifelong reminder of your need for God?

"God calls all of us to face our own brokenness. We can't make disciples for His Kingdom until we become disciples ourselves, fully submitting ourselves to His teaching, training, correction, and humbling in our own lives. We can't lead others where we have never been."

Tired of Trying, 184

4. In Hebrews 11, Jacob is included among those who are commended for persevering in their faith: "By faith Jacob, when he was dying, blessed each of Joseph's sons, and worshiped as he leaned on the top of his staff" (Hebrews 11:21). Having persevered in his wrestle and received God's blessings, Jacob could now pass those blessings on. Perhaps the mention of Jacob leaning on his staff is an acknowledgment that he was still dealing with that limp.

    Every choice we make to persevere—to obey, trust, and hold on to God despite the pain—contributes to the legacy of faith and blessing we leave to those around us. What comes to mind when you think about the legacy of faith and blessing you want to leave behind? Who are you willing to wrestle for?

A Blessing for All Who Wrestle

May you wrestle well.

May you courageously accept God's invitation
to hold on to Him through painful seasons.

May you be empowered to make hard
choices so you no longer feel stuck.

May you struggle well when the wrestle is
longer and harder than you expected.

May you see clearly the good that God
has always intended for you.

May you know, love, and trust your Savior
more than you ever have before.

May you walk boldly in the beauty of the
change He has brought to your life.

May your limp leave a legacy of faith and
blessing that no one can mistake for anything
but the mark of God on your life.

May you wrestle well.

NOTES

1. *Cambridge Dictionary*, s.v. "stuck (*adj.*)," accessed June 4, 2024, https://dictionary.cambridge.org/us/dictionary/english/stuck.
2. *Merriam-Webster*, s.v. "surrender (*v.*)," accessed May 24, 2024, https://www.merriam-webster.com/dictionary/surrender.
3. John H. Walton, *Genesis*, NIV Application Commentary Series, Terry Muck, gen. ed. (Grand Rapids, MI: Zondervan, 2001), 606.
4. Herbert Edward Ryle, "Genesis 32:28," *Cambridge Bible for Schools and Colleges*, Bible Hub, accessed May 30, 2024, https://biblehub.com/commentaries/cambridge/genesis/32.htm.
5. Ryle, "Genesis 32:28."
6. Walton, *Genesis*, 606.
7. John Gill, "Genesis 35:11," *John Gill's Exposition of the Entire Bible*, Bible Hub, accessed May 30, 2024, https://biblehub.com/commentaries/gill/genesis/35.htm.

ABOUT THE AUTHOR

Ashley Morgan Jackson is an author and speaker who has been ministering online through social media to her own community for over ten years. Formerly a senior social media and communications coordinator for Proverbs 31 Ministries, she continues to contribute by writing devotions and speaking at events, including the She Speaks conference for writers and the Reset conference, a one-day spiritual retreat. Ashley's ministry focus is communicating the grace and power of the truth of Christ and His Word to those whose faith feels fragile. She spent several years battling mental health issues and questioning why a God she had served her whole life was allowing such pain. Through her own wrestling, she found the blessing in being broken and now desires to share with others the beauty of allowing God to do what He has come to do in our lives.

Ashley resides in Charlotte, North Carolina, with her husband, Daniel. They have two school-age sons. Her daily prayer is that the joy of the Lord would be their strength. Ashley enjoys hanging out with her family, traveling, graphic design, prayer journaling, and laughing till she can't breathe.

Follow Ashley on Instagram, TikTok, and her website, ashleymorganjackson.com.

Reflections